Arctic Wolf

Children Book of Fun Facts & Amazing Photos on Animals in Nature - A Wonderful Arctic Wolf Book for Kids aged 3-7

By

Ina Felix

I'm an arctic wolf and I was born in the wild.

I live in a cold place called the Arctic.

I have a white thick fur to keep me warm.

My white thick fur helps me hide in the snow.

My white thick fur also prevents my skin from getting wet.

I have small ears and short legs.

My feet can walk in the cold snow.

My paws have fur to help me walk in the snow.

I like to be with other Arctic wolves.

I can see clearly and I can smell animals from far away.

I like to walk and search for food every day.

I have sharp teeth and powerful jaws.

I can run fast to catch animals and eat them.

I like to eat animals that are bigger than me.

I can live without eating for several days.

I dig the snow to make a home for my puppies.

I can give birth to 12 puppies.

My puppies cannot hear or see when they are born.

My puppies can hear and see after 12 days.

My puppies can also walk alone after 12 days.

I hope you had fun learning about my family.

Thank you.

Made in the USA
Middletown, DE
24 November 2019